Searching for the Spring

POETIC REFLECTIONS OF MAINE

by

Ken Nye

Freeport, Maine
2005

Published by TJMF Publishing

Library of Congress Control Number: 2005902909
ISBN: 0-9759314-8-2

Copyright © 2005 by TJMF Publishing

Poems in this book are the property of Kenneth P. Nye
knye@usm.maine.edu

Printed in the United States of America
by Fidlar Doubleday of Michigan
April, 2005

Designed by Scott Vile at the Ascensius Press, South Freeport, Maine
Cover photo: The Nye Farm, circa 1975

for Ken and Amy
and especially
for Ann

Table of Contents

Introduction

Someone told me once that
Einstein thought time is a variable.
That is to say
time is not a constant.

****

If Einstein was right,
and I think he was,
where is the throttle?
How do I slow this thing down?

WOW—a big idea captured in a few words, words that stand for something, that evoke, that illuminate. I've always thought that poetry is the French Impressionism of literature— the presentation of the essence of the thing without the sometimes distracting details. In this collection of poems rooted in Maine, Ken Nye paints lovely and sometimes haunting pictures—of places, people, and, especially, encounters with nature which always meets us on her own terms, rather than ours.

The poems are not esoteric or puzzling (as modern poetry so often is), but are really the opposite—they clarify and make manifest ideas and images we understand but had never seen so clearly. How about this line, for example, describing the memory of a lynx crossing the trail, but not seen by his son—

A beautiful silent micro movie in my head
that I can show to no one else.
Limited screenings
for the rest of my life.
Exclusive audiences only.
Just me.

Maine is the unmistakable setting for most of the work— the look of snow, the smells of a winter barn, the forests, or

". . . Katahdin, rising abruptly from the plane of lakes and trees, appearing almost nonchalant, as if it is unmoved by our looks of wonder." As in the previous line, Ken frequently finds ways to describe familiar sights and sounds (and smells) in ways which immediately register.

The poems meet my test—they'll make you smile, nod, and even generate the occasional Wow.

Gov. Angus King
July, 2004

Preface

I FIRST had the privilege of reading Ken Nye's poetry about a year ago, on an online writing site to which we both subscribed. Most of the poetry I read on the site was heartfelt and sincere, and while probably meaningful to its authors, seldom was it memorable enough to capture the attention of someone who reviewed more than one hundred poems a week. One fine day, I came across Ken's poem, "My Mother's Voice." As I read it, I held my breath. I had entered Ken's world, and my heart felt like it had come home.

Ken posted another poem. Then another. I soon discovered all of his poetry had a similar effect: A heart twinge, usually accompanied by the welling of tears. It didn't take me long to become a big fan of Ken's work. As I read, I often wondered, who is this poet who consistently evokes such strong emotion? How does he hit the poetic bulls-eye with such unerring accuracy?

In explanation, I could attempt a scholarly discussion on the merits of Ken's poetry, try to analyze how he employs imagery and metaphor to explore the natural world; show how his gently rambling and "prosey" style creates vignettes that are mini-vacations for the senses. But no technical exploration of Ken's writing can do it justice, just as no laundry list of someone's attributes can accurately capture their essence, nor explain why we love them. We just do. This is the realm of the heart, which has its own rationale, and no explanation, discussion, or justification holds sway. This is Ken's world, which he so graciously shares with us.

Some might categorize Ken solely as a New England poet. This is understandable. Certainly his poetry records—with the careful and painstaking detail of a naturalist—the beauty of his beloved Maine. Like a photographer or filmmaker, Ken captures the quiet dramas of Maine wildlife—squabbling between squirrels, the serenity of midnight snow, the rare and majestic appearance of an eagle. His poetry extols the virtues that characterize the Yankee spirit, qualities that make me proud to be a New Englander myself: ingenuity, self-reliance, fidelity, patriotism, love of neighbor, community and family. And always, that unbreakable connection to the land. But Maine's flora and fauna is only the backdrop of Ken's world, the vehicle for his heart poured out. The State of Maine may be his home, but you'll soon discover that Maine is also a state of mind . . . and of heart.

Like letters from home when you're far away, Ken's poems awaken within the reader a yearning for the simplicity, security, and rootedness of home. Each one is a snapshot, a memory of a place or relationship that affirms, provides a sense of history, identity and belonging. This is why I believe Ken Nye is more than just a New England poet, for these are American snapshots, visions of the American dream. In a sense, we are all searching for our spring. Luckily, Ken knows the terrain of the heart and generously leads us to water.

Come, friends, let us drink deeply.

LORRAINE SAUTNER
January 1, 2005

Foreword

MY HEART was first molded a Mainer's when I was five and my parents purchased land on Lake Androscoggin in Wayne where they built a summer camp. My father was a minister and, consequently, we always lived in homes that, as I saw it at the time, were loaned to us. But the camp in Wayne was ours. It has always been, and still is, the center of our family's life and the summer gathering point for family members who are spread out all over the eastern seaboard.

My wife Ann and I both graduated from Colby College in Waterville, Maine, and after seven years in temporary residence in the mid-west, we returned to Maine to raise our family and to become official residents. That was thirty-three years ago. We bought an old farm in Rumford Center, up toward Andover, that hadn't been lived in for five years, had hay growing right up to the front door, a hole in the back roof, an "L" and shed and attached barn that went on forever, five outbuildings in various stages of decay. We lived there for thirteen wondrous years, raised two children, a small herd of Black Angus cattle, chickens (and eggs), bees (and honey). We hiked the woods, climbed the cliffs, skied the snowmobile trails that could take us through the wilderness to Canada. We burned eight to ten cords of wood every winter (wood that we cut, split, hauled, and stacked ourselves), swam in the Ellis River all summer, fought the snow drifts every winter day to get out and later to get back in, rose every morning to the sun coming up over the cliff in back of our barn and went to bed every night to the glow of sunsets behind the mountain and cliffs on the other side of the valley.

When our slave labor force graduated from high school and went to live their lives as Mainers in other corners of the state, we reluctantly said farewell to the mountains and our farm and now enjoy coastal suburbia in Freeport. We still live in the country, (Maine doesn't really have a suburbia), in an 1830 New England center chimney cape with three fireplaces and a yard that is bordered by woods. We both are past our 60th birthdays, still working (Ann teaches in an elementary school, I teach at the University of Southern Maine), both dealing with health issues that have raised our appreciation of good health. (Ann has an implanted defibrillator; I have Parkinson's.) But we are grateful that we live in such a beautiful place, surrounded by family and the beauty of Maine.

One last note of possible interest: I began writing poetry two years ago when I wanted a way to tell Ann how much she meant to me. We have known each other since we were twelve and have been in love since we were seventeen. The poem "One Moment, One Lifetime" was the first poem I wrote. Having had fun composing it, and finding out that through poetry I can explore and express my feelings, I have been writing ever since. I don't attempt to hide the fact that my poetry is personal stuff, but that is what poetry should be. And, because it's personal is why I begin this collection with a little information about the person who wrote it.

I hope that by reading these poems you get to feel a little of the pervasive culture of Maine in which human beings find rejuvenation, inspiration, connection and strength from the mountains and forests and waters of this beautiful corner or our country.

KEN NYE

Maine's Natural World

SEARCHING FOR THE SPRING

I'd been told our spring water comes down the hill
through an underground pipe,
from "a spring by the wall, about 500 yards in back of the barn."

Expecting to simply go find the spring,
I head up the hill along the stone wall.
It's not easy going. Halfway up,
the impenetrable forest of scrub pines and firs
starts forcing me away from the wall.
Eventually, the wall, not the spring,
is the goal of my search.
Continuing up hill, I start angling left, then right,
broadening the length of my tack with each turn.
Eventually, though, it dawns on me:
I have no idea where I am.

I'm well more than 500 yards from the barn,
with no sign of wall, let alone spring.
Ahead there is more uphill forest to climb.
But facing down hill, just to my left,
I can see open sky through thick branches of brush.
Unsure of the reason for this hole in the forest,
I push through the bushes and
suddenly
the dark of the forest is gone
as I step onto a rock at the top of a cliff.

As if standing on a cloud,
I can see the river, the centerpiece of the valley,
meandering down from Andover,
the fields beyond the river,
the farm beyond the fields,
and the cliffs on the far side of the valley.
Below me, the trees are
a dance floor of green.
I'm tempted to spread my wings
and glide out over the forest.

3

I can just see the roof of our barn.
The rest of our farm is screened by the hill
on which I began the search for the spring.

I sit down and drink in this vista.
Then my eyes are drawn to the granite on which I sit.
Crystals of mica spiced throughout.
White, creamy and yellow quartz in abundance.
The rock is a masterpiece.
So is the view.

But this is something that has to be shared.
Tomorrow I'll bring the family up here.

And maybe later I'll find the spring.

And maybe not.

GOING HOME AT TWILIGHT *

Coming down the trail at twilight,
I am perilously close to
being stranded in darkness.
Earlier I had figured
I could ski the loop
before it got dark.
I was wrong.
But I know where I am,
and in the dwindling light
I see the trail, and the trail
will bring me home.

It is snowing hard.
When I stop, the only sound in the forest
is snow falling on snow.
About to push off
and begin the long downhill run
back to the logging road,
I hear just above my head
a sound like the comforter
being moved as my wife turns in her sleep.
I look up and see a huge snowy owl,
wings wide spread,
gliding down the same trail,
staying below the branches,
occasionally pumping huge wings
to navigate around a tree.
My eyes follow the owl down the glide path
until he disappears in the twilight and snow.

I am left alone in the growing darkness,
hearing again only the sound of snow,
wondering if the owl is going home, too.

Dedicated to the memory of my dear friend and neighbor,
Jane Holt deFrees
October 2, 2004

THE FAWN

Coming out of the pond, no need to towel off
in this warm afternoon sun.
I'll hike up through the orchard
on Grandpa's favorite trail.
(He loved to carve paths with his tractor,
his way of reclaiming the forest.)

I slip on my sneakers
and start up the path,
alone with my thoughts.
The freshly mown grass cushions my tread
as I soundlessly move up the hill.
I hear bees in blueberry blossoms,
a crow in the hollow, yelling at owls.
Otherwise, hardly a sound.

At the top, I follow the path
down the back of the hill
where it loops in return to the barn.
The apple trees here are competing with pines.
More confined than the orchard on top.

Following the trail, I step 'round a pine
as a fawn steps 'round the next apple.
We meet face to face and instantly freeze.
The only discernible movement —
his nose, twisting and flaring like mad,
seeking a hint of what I am.

I study him.
No more than a day or two old,
speckled with soft white spots,
he is, like all babies,
a beautiful miniature.
Hooves, tiny and perfectly shaped.
Slender, taughtly strung legs.
Hankie sized white tail

ready to flash the signal to run
should I move.
Ears, turned to pick up my sound.
Eyes, like marbles, taking me in.
Everything about him, flawless.

I am struck by the splendor of
afternoon sun
slanting through branches
to bless this child,
using all of his senses to ask who I am.
Feeling kinship with him, I wish we could touch
but know that our worlds won't allow it.

We stand for what seems a very long time,
and then off to the right, from behind a thick pine,
comes a clearly audible snort.
The fawn turns and steps through the pine boughs,
heading off with his mom to the gully.

I am in awe of what just happened —
still trailing clouds of glory,
this purely innocent baby being,
looked in my eyes
and weighed my goodness.

THE LYNX

Cross country skiing with my son,
working up a sweat trying to stay in front.
It's a classic mid-winter day
in Maine —
deep blue sky,
air sharply crisp and clear,
temperature in the mid teens,
a soft Chinook-like breeze
sliding down the mountain side
brushing our faces.
Brilliantly white, the fresh snow sparkles
like a Christmas card and occasionally
swirls in the wind.

We are on an abandoned logging road
with the mountain on our left
and the downhill on our right,
heavy woods on both sides of the trail.
Reaching the top of a long uphill run,
I stop and turn to say I'm tired,
just as a lynx
flies out of the woods
20 yards back down the trail
and in one leap disappears
into the trees on the other side.
Not a sound.
The image appears and disappears in a second.
I point and whisper-shout,
"Quick, Ken, look!"
But when he turns, the trail is empty.

I want him to have seen the lynx.
I tell him excitedly what I saw,
hoping my telling of it
will match the real thing.
He is patient,
but I can tell the image is not there.

I cannot recreate that split second for him.
I am running the film over and over in my head,
but I can't project it into his.

I consider telling it frame by frame —
A magnificent wild cat in the downward arc of
the leap from the woods, the landing, the coil,
the upward arc
of the leap
into the woods.
Then nothing.
It's gone.

But slow motion won't work.

A beautiful silent micro movie in my head
that I can show to no one else.
Limited screenings for the rest of my life.
Exclusive audiences only.
Just me.

But I wish my son had seen it with me.

We turn the corner and head up the trail.

STARS IN HER POCKET

Millions lie before her.
She overlooks most, but here is one
that warrants inspection.
Something in the smooth roundness of the glistening wet stone
catches her eye,
like a shooting star.
Stooping, she plucks it from the foaming sand,
holds it in her hand,
rolls it over,
examines its veins
and blended colors.
But it lacks something.
She discards it
and begins again to scan the stars before her,
washed every few seconds
by an infinite number of swirling eddies,
one after the other, as she searches for the perfect stone.

Here is one of unusual...........What?
What is it about this stone
that gets her attention?
What is it
that refuels the possibility of selection?
A color that echoes a chord in her memory?
A design in the miracle mix of magma and malachite?
An elevation of the thrill of discovery,
the wonder of the limitless galaxy of miniature globes,
fresh and pure,
perennially washed and waiting for her?

She will do this all afternoon
and end up with a pocket
pulling the side of her shorts into a sag.
Returning to the blanket, she will disgorge the stars
onto a terry cloth towel and sit and gaze at them,
as one contemplates the heavens
on a crisp, moonless night in deep winter.

Chalice of mysteries,
each stone an untold story of creation,
journey,
infinite age,
flawless beauty even in its abundance.

Millions lie before her,
yet it is only these that she has chosen.
Do they recognize the honor?
Will they ever again,
in the infinite eons of time,
be judged worthy of wonder?

THE JACK-IN-THE-PULPIT

Children's story books
color forests
green.
I look around me
in the shadowed under story
of this wilderness trail,
and see touches of it
here and there.

Mostly, though, I see brown —
dried leaves,
decomposed twigs,
tree bark that no longer has
a tree to contain and now lies
useless,
waiting to dissolve into the
dirt, dust and detritus
of the forest floor.

Lifelessness surrounds me —
dead trees,
limbs hanging useless
like broken legs on a racehorse,
rotting acorns and pine cones,
sodden piles of leaves everywhere,
rotten logs,
some having been disemboweled
by bears, fishers or raccoons
foraging for protein.

This rich reservoir of decay
seems irrefutable evidence that all things die.
Kind of a depressing conclusion to take away
from a hike in the woods.

But, as I survey
this silent woodland sanctuary,
my attention is drawn to a Jack-in-the-pulpit,
standing resolutely amid a pile of leaves,
and I again start to see the color green,
not rolled out in broad strokes,
but scattered splotches of vibrant color:
pristine fleece-like mosses
beneath my feet
covering damp rocks and decaying limbs;
curled harp-like heads of green ferns
thrusting up through the nutrient-rich loam
of the forest floor;
saplings "nursed" by
the remains of mighty pine trees of years past
that are now only
decomposing giants lying on the ground.
Everywhere I look,
I see new, green life growing out of
brown dead things.

And, as I stand and allow the hushed
silence of the deep forest
to envelope me,
this forest glade becomes an ancient Norman chapel,
a holy refuge,
with sunbeams slicing through
the vernal shadows
to reveal,
not a museum of skeletons from ages past,
but a natural nursery in which
the old, the dead, and the dying
give themselves to nurture and sustain
the young, the living and the new.

SUMMER STORM

On my knees in the garden,
pushing cedar shingles into the soil
around new tomato plants
to protect them from the wind and careless dogs,
I fish a black fly out of my ear in pieces.

Lost in thought, I am barely aware
of a strange sound in the distance.
But, as it grows louder and nearer,
I look up and experience momentary panic
when the world suddenly makes no sense.
Down the valley the sky is black,
and the air is solid water.
The storm cloud,
already engulfing
the mountain on the far side of the valley,
is roiling straight toward our house.
I can see a wall of water advancing up the road.
Nothing will stop this storm
from marching right over our farm
and continuing up the valley toward the Notch.

I run to the tractor, intent on keeping the
old machine dry,
(as if it had never been wet before).
It reluctantly cranks over and starts to sputter
as the first raindrops hit.
But these are not drops of water;
these are balls of water.

I floor the accelerator and bolt to the barn.
Already soaked to the skin,
I stand in the doorway and
watch the storm scour our valley.
Lightning and thunder add to the show,
with rain so heavy the water flows over the ground
like a high tide pushed into alien territory by a storm surge.

The wind gusts blow the water horizontally.
My cedar Stonehenge shields
around the tomato plants are flattened,
in some cases flattening the plants as they go down.

In a few minutes the rain eases up,
and I sense the sky lighten.
Then, as quickly as it came,
the storm is gone,
and our valley is utterly silent.

The late afternoon sun
slices through clouds still lingering in the west,
creating slanting paths of light here and there,
as if a bank of spotlights were installed in the clouds,
directed to highlight mundane things:
a clump of alders in the pasture,
the cliff on the mountain behind our farm.
I expect to see a trapeze artist in tights
step up to the edge of the cliff and,
with a graceful gesture to the audience,
ask for applause.

One beam zeroes in on mud puddles in the driveway,
revealing designs in the sand
shaped by the winds of the storm.
Another highlights a bed of asparagus shoots,
just breaking through the surface
from their roots two feet down.
Everywhere I turn are beacons of light,
as if I'm in a gem shop with
God's miracles on display.

One spotlighted showcase after another
as the clouds that aim the light beams
continue to boil toward the notch in the mountains.

Then the clouds are gone,
the house lights come up.
The world has been washed clean.

In need of dry clothes, I walk to the house.
Steam rises from the ground.
A barn swallow, taking advantage of the storm,
streaks out of the open window in the loft
to pluck grubs from
the warm moist dirt in the garden
to feed to her brood in the rafters.

Life goes on,
but the world is new.
And my heart is charged by the power of the storm
and the display of the miracles around me.

WILDERNESS SERENADE

No matter where I find it,
clear water flowing over pristine sand and gravel
always stirs in me a longing for wilderness,
empty forests, dark and foreboding,
with small streams searching their way
from mountainside to ocean,
banks lined with moss,
rocks covered with wet green growth
that makes me pay attention to my step,
sunlight reaching the forest floor
only in sunbeams.

When I was a boy in New York
walking home from school
along Quaker Road,
a drainage ditch, lined with sand and
looking like a bubbling spring in a
Maine forest,
was, to me, the picture of vernal purity.
Never mind the paper cups here and there,
the orphaned hub cap and occasional Twinkie wrapper
caught in the current.
Even now, fifty years afterwards,
I can conjure a clear image
of that roadside drainage ditch
that called to me, like a siren.

Now, when I roam the foothills
of the White Mountains of Maine,
I am conscious of
the sentinel silence of heavy woods,
broken occasionally by distant cries of crows,
and then by the soft, cheerful cadence
of water flowing from pool to pool,
a whispered serenade, played by the natural world.
Making their stepped journeys down stairways
built by glaciers,

along streambeds lined with white sand
and peppered with tiny water-logged pine cones,
these primitive vessels of nature's life blood
create an almost inaudible music
for lovers of the forests' wonders.

Coming upon a brook in the middle of wilderness,
I always wonder where it begins,
where it ends,
what I would find if I followed it
up or down.

A few times I have come upon the origin of
one of these pristine tendrils of purity,
a mid-forest swamp,
carpeted with skunk cabbage and marsh weed,
an oasis of watery green in the dark under story.
Footprints here and there —
deer, moose, raccoon, coyote —
all drawing life from a watery nursery.
And, inevitably, I search at the edge of the
swamp for the outflow,
the beginning of another forest capillary
carrying life
and sustenance
to unknown corners
of the forest.

There is a mystery in a mountain stream.
Like gazing at a fire,
I am mesmerized by its simple beauty
and only feel the questions
whose answers are yet to be discovered.

GOLD IS A COLOR

Storybook fables give gold a rich luster
that loses its brilliance with closer inspection.

Colors of leaves in autumn's bright showcase
make my heart race and fill me with wonder.
But the gold doesn't last,
(like the red and the yellow)
and all become compost that cries for attention,
a layer of brown on
my once perfect lawn.

Brushstrokes of gold in the beauty of sunsets
thrill me with wonder of artful design.
But in minutes the sun, the source of the treasure,
continues its journey below the horizon,
and the gold of the sunset becomes
evening, then night.

Wherever I look I see gold effervescing,
first calling attention to brightness and bounty
but losing its beauty as time moves along.

So, counting my wealth in the color of gold,
I've learned that, while pretty, its luster will fade.
Though I thrill to its beauty, I know that real wealth
is the love that we share in a world full of wonder,
and that gold is a color,
nothing more, nothing less.

REMEMBERING THE FARM

My nose sometimes
catches something floating by that has a trace
of a farm smell:

Pine scent wafting down the hillside
in early evening,
filling the door yard
with an invisible mist of cleanliness and purity,
a reminder that our farm
is on the edge of wilderness.

The musty odor of
cobwebs,
spider ropes fifty years old,
dust deep as dirt
blanketing
horse harnesses and farm implements
from an era now gone.

The smell of hay,
still fresh and clean,
in the empty barn.
But in a corner of the loft,
the hay is scented with musty dust
that intermingles with the flavor
of new cut grass.

Thunderstorm nitrogen,
floating up from the pasture
after a mid-July lightning show,
bringing in its wake
the rich earthy smell
of wet soil
and cow dung.

The sinus-filling aroma of a wood stew
percolating up
from the ten cords
of freshly split hardwood,
stacked floor to ceiling in the basement.

The odor of fresh warm milk,
now puddling on the floor,
as I press my face into the side of a Black Angus
and, with one hand,
pull one of the cow's teats and,
with the other, drag her reluctant giant newborn
to his first breakfast.

The smell of burning chicken feathers,
evoking images of beheadings
and eviscerations,
eyes of chickens still blinking
as heads without bodies
pile up at the base of the wood block.

But the smell that I will cherish is
the smell of the kitchen,
a potpourri of wood smoke,
damp dog hair,
dinner on the stove,
winter jackets, still wet from the storm,
and the people who wear them –
the smells of family and farm.

C'EST LA VIE

While doing the morning dishes,
I watch the chickadees in the back yard
flit back and forth
from one feeder to another,
creating roller coaster flight patterns
that remind me of the
country roads of Nebraska.
Directly beneath my window on the bulkhead
is a red squirrel,
one of the squatters inside the walls of our
old New England cape.
(Talk about domestic strife! They need counseling.)
While the squirrel loses himself in a morning wash up,
two humming birds zoom in to the sugar water feeder,
confront each other
with loud epithets and threatening feints
and then disappear
when one concedes defeat and zips away,
immediately followed by the other
who apparently has more to say.
Lost in thought, the squirrel is oblivious to
a butterfly tiptoeing through the blossoms on the deck.

Suddenly a hawk,
streaking down from the left
of my view,
whirls around between the porch and the house
with his full wing span spread and
then charges straight at my window
to snatch the red squirrel from the bulkhead.
At the last instant the squirrel leaps down to the deck
and loses only a tuft of hair.
Disgusted, the hawk pauses momentarily,
(as if considering going under the deck after the squirrel)
spreads his wings, and
powers up through the trees
out of sight.

I am stunned.
In the yard there is total silence.
No wildlife anywhere,
all scattering to hidden places.

But in less than a minute,
a chickadee from a neighbor's feeder,
oblivious to the attempted kill only a few minutes before,
innocently drops onto a feeder perch.
Immediately the local denizens rise to the challenge,
reappear at the feeder.
The red squirrel ventures out from the bulkhead,
followed by an irate cousin who cusses him
and initiates a frenetic chase around the back deck.
They disappear into the pachysandra.
The butterfly skips back into view,
hop-scotching from flower to flower,
tasting the nectar.

I am struck by the apparent indifference
of these wild things to the explosive
threat of death like I just
witnessed from my kitchen window.

But, as the feathered neighborhood
swarms back to the feeder,
I see a chickadee on a feeder perch,
pausing just momentarily,
as if pondering the events of the last few minutes,
shrugging his shoulders and
muttering "C'est la vie,"
as he pulls another sunflower seed
from the feeder tube.

Lesson learned.

THE INDIGO BUNTING

Watching the traffic at the bird feeder
could get boring
for some people, I guess.
But it never does for me.
There is always the possibility of the arrival of
a show stopper.

I must admit that seeing goldfinches
day after day eventually dulls the excitement
over seeing a yellow bird.
But goldfinches are strikingly beautiful.
And when they arrive in numbers,
their colorful comings and goings
are mesmerizing.

Usually, travelling with the goldfinches,
are purple finches.
Not as eye catching as their yellow cousins,
but their reddish purple hue,
mixed with the bright yellow of the goldfinches,
produces a feathered technicolor bouquet
for the breakfast window.

The black and white of the chickadees and nuthatches
and the soft grays of the titmice,
while not contributing to the rainbow at the feeder tubes,
add richness and animation to the canvas.

And every once in a while, two cardinals,
who reside down the road,
stop in to check the freshness of our sunflower seeds.
The addition of the bright red of the male cardinal
and the muted mustard of the female to our breakfast palette
creates a surprisingly entrancing alternative to the "Today Show."

One morning four years ago,
I looked out,
and amidst the rainbow at the feeder
was a brilliantly blue angel with wings.
It was an indigo bunting, a bird rarely seen in Maine.
As I quietly called my wife in to see this breathtaking tableau,
I was reminded of Michaelangelo's *Last Supper*.
Although the indigo bunting was just one more bird
added to the banquet scene,
our eyes were drawn to it as if it wore a halo.

Nature was offering us a picture that morning
to remind us that beauty in the world
occurs in myriad places at unexpected times,
in random order and without introduction.
And that the morning show outside the window
can be more beautiful and spirit enhancing
than the shows sent our way on the air waves of technology.

THE HERMIT

If you look carefully as you go up
the Howard Pond Road
you can see the remains of an old mansion
in the woods off to the left at the end
of a long overgrown driveway.
There was a time when it didn't look so decrepit,
when it had "possibilities."
Our friends were thinking of buying it and restoring it.
"Let's walk up and take a look."

A beautiful autumn day:
yellow, gold and red brown leaves everywhere,
some still clinging to branches,
others somersaulting through the air,
swept into mini cyclones by the brisk autumn wind.

Walking up the road
we wave at friends driving by on their way into town.
We arrive at the abandoned driveway, and,
shuffling through leaves, start down.

It's a golden tunnel.
The morning sunlight slants through the yellow trees,
not just highlighting the splendor of the autumn colors
but sharpening the image of every object
before us.
Up ahead, off to the side of the path,
is a heap of leaves,
appearing almost as if someone
had raked them into a pile,
but common sense
tells us that it's simply
a creation of the natural world.
No one would have tried
to rake the leaves on this abandoned road.

As we get closer,
we can see that it's not a pile of leaves;
it's a rock that was never moved
completely from the road.
The leaves have simply blanketed it.

Then suddenly the rock moves.

We all stop, unsure of this mysterious hulk
huddled as if to spring.
From out of the bottom of the pile of leaves
slowly appears a human leg.
"My god!" someone utters.

We approach cautiously,
but the person under those leaves is not aware
of our presence.
"Is he asleep?" someone asks.
"I think he's unconscious."
"Who is this?"

The head moves.
It is as if we are watching a chrysalis open.
A face appears, slowly turns toward us.
Eyes awakening from slumber or stupor
focus slowly,
scan our circle,
trying to piece together an explanation
for his being on the ground
and our presence and looks of concern.

He attempts to get up
but cannot.
Two of us reach out and support his arms
as he continues to try to rise.
We ask him gently who he is.
As he stands on wobbly legs
he says that he's been living
in the mansion,

but the well ran dry.
He was on his way to town to get a drink of water.
He fell on the path and couldn't get up.
"How long have you been here?"
"I don't know."
We don't learn much about him.
He is very old.
And he is sick and confused.

Our excursion to the old mansion
becomes a trip to the hospital where we pass
to the medical community this
hermit who needed a drink of water.

A few days after this incident
we see him on the sidewalk in town,
looking better than when we left him.
But three months after we found him
on the path
he died.

Two worlds converged in that yellow wood,
and, still, I wonder why.

HEADING SOUTH

Autumn, late afternoon,
hauling the front storm door
up from the barn,
I hear dead oak leaves
still on branches
rustling in the breeze.
Then, in the distance,
rhythmic cries,
like a coxswain
in a far off racing shell.

As the sound gets closer,
I step into the middle of the lawn
to get a more expansive view of the sky.
Looking north, I can see them coming,
a wing of Canada geese,
pumping to a cacophony of rhythms,
but all maintaining the formation,
each staying in the draft of the one ahead.
Only the leader
has no one in front
to ease his task.

I stand and watch them pass over.
Then, wishing I had someone in front of me
to make the storm door lighter,
I resume my own journey south.

SUMMER TWICE

March comes in like a lion in Maine
and goes out in much the same mood.
Leaning against the wind and sleet,
I remind myself, "We're almost there.
Only a couple of months to go!"

And as mid-march coils into late-March and
late-March springs into April,
more and more of my free moments are lost
in visions of summer that shimmer in my head.

I live a Maine summer twice —
first in a winter-long dream of the summer to come,
a succession of adventures
in my mind
while snow still covers the ground.

I wake up at dawn to a cloudless sky
and a promise of summer heat,
go down to the foot of the drive for the paper
and talk to the swallows lined up on the wire.
(I like to think that they sense I'm friendly,
even if they don't understand what I say.)
I ride my bike down to my boat at the harbor,
remove the windscreens and then just sit.
Maybe I go for a ride.
Maybe not.

We go on all kinds of myriad adventures:
Monhegan Island, a whale watch, Quebec.

I buy a small pool for my granddaughters and friends,
relish their screams of joy and delight.
(And when mid-summer heat becomes more than I want,
in the dark of night the pool becomes mine.)

Then summer comes.
We don't do all I dreamed.
I sleep later than I should.
It rains, sometimes for days.

But we rediscover year after year
that the joy of a Maine summer
comes less from what we do
and more from how we feel.

Storms at the lake with curtains of rain.
Wind gusts we can see beginning their charge
from across the water
thrill us with indiscriminate power.
Trying to beat the storm,
we scramble to secure the deck, close the windows,
pull the boats up and then
stand at the front windows of the camp
and watch the storm transform the world.

Sunsets over the western mountains
renew our awareness of
the spirit of life.

Summer heat
rekindles the passion of romance,
rising Phoenix-like
from the memories of summers past.

Let it snow, let it blow.
I'm in summer mode.
And when summer comes and simmers our days
with blue sky soaked with sunlight
and brushes our nights
with pine scented zephyrs
of cool air from the mountain behind us,
I will be grateful
that I have summer
twice.

THE COUNTY

Traveling north, we see nothing but trees,
millions of them.
Hemlocks, pines, spruce, cedars, junipers.
The landscape everywhere is ever green,
peppered with splotches of light brown grass and wetland,
setting off the trees like a camel hair vest
highlights a green holiday shirt.
Occasionally, the naked, whiskered limbs
of a tamarack are visible,
like dead wood amidst arboreal greenery.
And white birches appear here and there, but,
unless they are many,
their beauty is muted by the emerald sea around them.

Miles of primeval woodlands and suddenly,
off to the west looms Katahdin,
rising abruptly from the plane of lakes and trees,
appearing almost nonchalant,
unmoved by our looks of wonder.
We keep looking over our left shoulders
as the mountain that will stay forever wild slips behind us.
Eventually the view reverts to the awesomely endless forest.

Having grown accustomed to the plethora of trees,
we are almost unaware of the change in landscape
to less heavily forested, rolling hills.
Signs of human endeavor begin to appear.
On distant hillsides we see farms and the patchwork
of potato and hay fields.
We are entering the "other Maine,"
the part of the state that sits on the
other side of the evergreen wilderness
we just traversed.

This is "The County,"
a place with a heart all its own,
a feel of the familiar even to strangers.
We pass through nondescript villages with homes
clustered around a fire station and convenience store,
each town welcoming us to their village
proudly,
almost defiantly,
declaring their existence in spite of the
"For Sale" signs planted in front lawns.

Stopping to buy some potatoes, we are introduced
to grocery shopping by the honor system —
"Please leave your money in the metal box.
If you can't find the correct change,
please knock on the door of the house.
If no one answers,
please take an amount of change
that is closest to what you need."
Looking around, we cannot discern
where the security camera is hidden.
It's like stopping in to see your sister
only to find a note that says,
"Hi. I thought you might stop by.
There are lemon squares in the refrigerator."

As we drive deeper into the County,
we don't see smokestacks
or other structures indicative of heavy industry,
or effluents from polluters flowing into
pristine rivers.
Other than potato businesses,
there is little industry wherever we go.

We wonder, "What do people do up here?"
The answer, we eventually learn, is:
they farm,
they haul,
they search for ways to make ends meet.

They dream,
they plan for better days.
They share their burdens and support their friends.
They nurture their little ones.
They don't lock their doors.
They are an unpretentious people,
hospitable but not effusively so.
They seem to assume that a visitor has good reason
to be there, but what that reason is
is none of their business.
They are strong on common sense
and rely on the world staying pretty much
just like it was yesterday.
If you become a friend, it's a lifetime membership.
You won't be considered a visitor after that.
A conversation interrupted two years past
is continued, as if punctuated with a dash rather
than a blank page and a new chapter title.

In the County, all are family.
Someone's sister-in-law
is related to someone else's uncle.
Even new arrivals have ties
to the County about which they were totally unaware.

The land is starkly but beautifully barren.
The sky is open,
tinged with pastels,
limited only by the horizon above the trees or fields
in every direction.
There is a feeling of freedom in this environment,
of cleanliness
and godliness
and security.

We used to wonder, "Why do people stay up here?"
Now we ask, "Why do people leave?"

There should be a sign on 95 in Houlton that says,
"Welcome to the County,
where the state of Maine comes
to learn the way life should be."

*Written in celebration
of the Graduation of the Class of 2004,
University of Southern Maine
Ed. Leadership Master's Program*

Presque Isle, Maine

May 7, 2004

A NOISE AT THE WINDOW

Sitting at the computer, I hear a dull thud at the window.
It is morning and the bird feeder in the garden is a frenzy.
I suspect a goldfinch,
giving up its spot on a feeder perch,
mistook the garden reflected in my window
for the real thing.
Going to the window, I look out on the ground.
It's a chickadee, not a goldfinch.
But, whatever,
it's a shame.
What a sad thing, to fly into the garden that is not there.
I go back to my work at the computer.

Later I check to see if the bird has revived.
Still there. Life has flicked off.
In the snap of a finger,
the click of a light switch,
the garden disappeared.

I return to the computer in the dark corner,
remembering the sound at the window.

LOOKING FOR EAGLES

Our lake is a bird watcher's paradise.

Strikingly beautiful during the day
in their black and white tuxedos,
loons extend their presence at night
with their haunting hooting and yodeling.

Osprey nests are visible in tall pines,
scattered at appropriate intervals around the lake
to preserve harmony in the fishing community.

On the surrounding hillsides,
crows keep up a seemingly endless cacophany of noise,
making me wonder what it is in their world
that prompts such an endless racket.
I sometimes think they think their calls
are an accompaniment to the goings on of the natural world,
like organ music accompanies a soap opera.
You don't really hear it unless you focus your attention on it,
and if you do, you don't like it.

Sea gulls, riding the wind currents that swirl over the lake,
constantly scan the water surface for dying fish or edible debris.
Lovely to watch as they slide from breeze to breeze,
they hang motionless, like kites without strings.
But they perch on swim floats,
leaving a mess that takes the romance
out of a dip in the lake.
Most of us wish they stayed up in the air.

But the bird that is only rarely seen and that brings people
out of the cottage on the run to glimpse
is the eagle.

So rarely do we see an eagle,
we plan daylong excursions to go find one.
We climb in the canoe,
head down the lake toward Lothrop Island
where the eagles have built two huge nests.
As we paddle, we keep our eyes
on distant specks in the sky that,
on closer inspection,
may be eagles.
There are always birds over
or around the lake,
and, with binoculars close at hand,
we usually rise to the challenge of
sorting out who is who.

From a distance, even sea gulls
can masquerade as raptors.
And soaring crows, riding the thermals over the forest,
catch our attention,
until a big eagle-like bird
heads directly toward us
and we get excited.
As it passes over, we see the white
circles on the underside of the wings —
an osprey,
large and stately,
but not projecting the majesty of an eagle.

Then, suddenly, appearing over the southern end of Norris Island,
still a long way off, appears a bird so big it dwarfs
all the others.
Pumping massively powerful wings every once in a while,
it rides the wind currents
that slide around the island on their way down the lake.
There is no wondering if this is an eagle.
It is huge, looking almost prehistoric in its pendulous
sweep of wings.

From three hundred feet above the pines on the island,
it surveys its realm,
like a monarch assessing the condition of his kingdom
from atop a castle tower.
We get the feeling, as we watch this regal
ruler of the waters,
that this is an animal that fears nothing.
Even at this distance,
we can sense its power,
the strength in its talons,
the will to rule these islands,
not ruthlessly,
but unquestionably.

We continue down the lake toward Lothrop
and the nests, hoping the eagle is going in the same direction.

As we approach the island,
we see the two nests in the tops of dead pine trees.
More like a tree house than a nest,
weighing more than a ton,
each nest is a platform built of sticks and mud
and functions like the deck of an aircraft carrier.
We see the white heads of two eagles
who have spotted us and
warn us away
with noisy epithets.
We sense that these are young eagles
who wish mom or dad was around to take care of these intruders.

As if responding to their calls to return home,
the eagle we had first seen over Norris
swoops up into view from the backside of the island
and eases itself down onto to the landing pad,
perches on the edge of the nest, and
silently glares at us, like a teacher
who controls a study hall simply with her stare.

We back away, understanding the eagle's demeanor clearly.
We head back up the lake,
having accomplished our goal.

There will be other days when we feel a need
to touch this world of majesty.
But each time we enter the eagles' realm,
we leave with a memory that never fades.

CAMP

Summers spent at a lakeside cottage
brand the memory lobe —
experiences fifty years old,
but I see them still,
as vivid and sharp as looking in
a Viewfinder.

Dad's a different person at camp.
When he makes pancakes
on the griddle,
we sit there,
a jug of local maple syrup in the middle of the table,
hurry to finish the pancakes left on our plates,
so we can claim another pile,
an excuse to pour on more of the golden elixir
until Mom says, "That's enough."
Breakfast the next day
is a cereal free-for-all in the kitchen,
while Mom and Dad sit out on the deck
and Dad barbecues chunks of sausage, ham,
and pineapple
over a tiny cast iron kettle cooker
that he has carefully
stoked with strips of birch bark.

The memory of Dad sitting out there
nursing his miniature
roasting pit right on the deck table,
testing the degree of doneness of each mouthful-sized
piece of sausage will be with me forever.

We boys sleep on the "sleeping porch"
in military green army surplus bunk-beds
on one wall, and on the other
in navy surplus fold-down beds,
suspended by chains and folded up against
the wall every morning.

(These navy bunks have special appeal —
they came out of the
Liberty Ships of the recently ended world war.)
Nights on the sleeping porch,
with two of its four walls made
only of screening,
is sleeping in a tent.
Only a few feet from the lake,
we are lulled to sleep by the soothing sound
of the waves lapping up on the beach.

There are loons on our lake.
At night they hoot and yodel.
Friends brought up with us
from New York
hear those eerie calls
and burrow deeper into their sleeping bags.
In the morning the loons
sail across our swimming area,
stately and swan-like,
their black and white giving them
the appearance of painted toy sailboats.
In time, the haunting calls of the loons
become, for our friends as well as us,
part of the mystique
and romance of being at camp.

We play cards every night, Dad too.
A fire in the Franklin stove,
Mom knitting over on the sofa
or cooking something up for tomorrow,
everybody else at the dining table.
Usually we play Hearts, and
we know that some time
during the evening Dad is going to try to "shoot the moon."
He usually does it, too. Ticks me off.
Every time I try it, somebody gives
somebody else a heart

and I get all the rest of them…
plus the queen.
Ticks me off.

The camp has its own smell —
a combination of pine paneling,
moth balls,
cedar chests,
soggy dog hair,
wood smoke.

I love it.

It is feelings that color these memories:
Security of family and friends,
anticipation when waking to a day
loaded with possibilities of adventure
and fun,
mystery in the woods
and wonder of the world.

"Oh, don't you want to go,
to that promised land
where all is peace?
Oh, deep river, Lord,
I'm crossing over Jordan into campground."

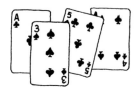

CLIMBING KATAHDIN

Up at dawn. No shower. No shave.
A jelly donut at the quik stop on the corner
and then on the road.
At the gate a little before 6:00,
we thread through
and head for
the Roaring Brook Trail parking area.

The weather is perfect —
late September, clear sky, temperature in the 50's
some leaves already down.

We put on hiking boots,
fill water bottles,
gather together for one final head count,
sign in at the ranger station
and begin up the trail.
Conversation is muted.
Heavy breathing develops in the first few minutes
as we all wait for our second wind to kick in.
We sound like a bunch of pack horses
as we wheeze and snort and clear our nasal passages.

The ascent is gradual.
After an hour, we sit on rocks and stumps for a break,
dig out snacks and water.
A lone woman hiker with a cane passes through.
We say good morning, but as she goes by
I wonder how she is going to make it to the summit.
She has a pronounced limp and relies heavily on the cane.
I feel a little smug, sure in my ability to make it to the top,
questioning hers.

Back on the trail, we overtake and pass the woman with the cane.
After another hour, another break.
Again the woman with the cane passes through
as we take our rest.
I wonder if she ever stops.

We reach Chimney Pond in late morning.
Feels good to see the summit
directly above us — way above us.
It's almost a mile and a half,
straight up.

After a light lunch at pond side,
and after smiling and waving again
at the woman with the cane
(doesn't she ever sit and rest?),
we begin the final ascent
up the Cathedral Trail.

The Cathedral Trail follows a huge rock slide
that thousands of years ago broke off the edge of the summit
plateau.
Hardly a "trail;"
more an obstacle course straight up.
Climbing from one huge broken boulder
to another,
we become absorbed in our individual
efforts to get up and over the next rock
in front of us.

I am wearing my Red Sox hat
with a broad front bill,
have it pulled
down close to my eyebrows to cut the glare.
Finding footholds for both feet
in the side of a boulder,
I prepare to heave myself up to the top.
But because of the long bill on my hat,
I don't see the overhang of the adjoining boulder
that protrudes down to where I am headed.
I hoist myself up head first
into the underside of the overhang.

As Sancho says in ""Man of la Mancha,"
"Whether the pitcher hits the stone
or the stone hits the pitcher,
it's going to be bad for the pitcher."
Works the same with a head.

I am stunned and almost lose sense of where I am.
I immediately feel a trickle of blood starting down
the side of my head.
My companions can see I have a problem
and all converge on my boulder.
Someone digs out a first aid kit,
cream is applied, bandages slapped on,
and then, with no more sympathy or attention,
I continue up the boulders.

Half way up, I pause, turn around and sit on the boulder.
I am amazed that I haven't had a problem with vertigo.
We are way up in the air, on a very steep incline.
I am pleased with myself.

We continue our climb up the rock slide
and in an hour and a half we arrive at the lip
of the summit plateau.
Katahdin is a huge flat topped monolith
that rises up out of the plain of forests, wetlands
and lakes of northern Maine.
Not a part of a chain of mountains,
it resembles
Ayers Rock in Australia,
a lone monster on the horizon
surrounded by flat wilderness.

Standing on the flat table top plateau,
we are not far from Baxter Peak,
the official "summit."
There is a crowd of people up there,
and we excitedly head in that direction.

We gather at the marker
indicating the official end
of the Appalachian Trail.
Cameras are brought out to document our achievement,
but our self-congratulations is muted by the arrival
of a small group of hikers who are completing
a three month trek that began on Stone Mountain
in Georgia.
We stand in awe of what they have done.
Their joy and sense of achievement overpower them.
There is no yelling for joy, no dancing a jig.
Instead, they walk over to the official marker of trail's end
and touch it reverently,
almost worshipfully,
tears streaking down cheeks.
We are all moved.
Somebody starts clapping and it catches on
until we are all part of a standing ovation on the summit
of Mt. Katahdin.
Then conversations begin, handshakes are exchanged,
and we all celebrate, both the achievements of others
and our own accomplishment.

After a light lunch and a nap,
we gather to begin the descent.
The plan was to go down via the Knife Edge,
across to Pomola Peak.
As we approach the Knife Edge and begin
to get a view of where we are headed,
bells start going off in my head.
The Knife Edge is aptly named.
Approximately 500 yards across,
it narrows at some points to a width of
three feet,
with 2500 foot drop-offs on either side.
The vertigo that I expected to strike me
on the Cathedral Trail manifests itself here.
I stop dead in my tracks and realize
I cannot do this.

Disappointed, embarrassed, but relieved,
I tell my companions that I will go back down
via the Saddle Trail and will meet them at the cars.
Seeing the look on my face, they don't try to dissuade me.
They continue out on to the Knife Edge
while I turn back toward the summit
and then head off across the plateau to the head
of the Saddle Trail.

I am about to step off the lip of the plateau
and onto the Saddle Trail when a figure
appears out of the shrubs that line the trail.
It is the woman with the cane,
only just now arriving on to the plateau.
She recognizes me and with a grin says, "I made it!"
I extend my hand to help her up on to the flat.
We hug.
I am speechless.
Without any conversation, she continues on
toward the summit.
I step down and begin my descent.

By dusk we have all reassembled in the parking lot.
We are tired,
but we sense that we are now somehow different.
We talk about the awesome view from the plateau,
about the standing ovation on the summit.
I inwardly reflect on the woman with the cane
whom I will never forget.
But the feeling that glows in me even now
is the self-satisfaction of having climbed Katahdin.

MONHEGAN MAIN STREET AT DAWN

Walking down Main Street on Monhegan at dawn,
I am in another time.
Not really a street —
more a broad dirt path
worn clean of roots and rocks
by three hundred years of footsteps.

Dawn on Monhegan marks the beginning of the work day.
When the sun rises, early or late,
fishermen rise with it.
Just as diesel bus smoke gives dawn
on Broadway the flavor of commerce,
the aroma of coffee in this predawn twilight
wafts along Monhegan Main Street,
coloring the soft pastels of the land —
the gardens and meadows and fishermen's houses —
with a hazy satin finish and a palpable taste
of breakfast on the stove,
read by the nose instead of the eyes.

In the corner snack shop,
locals and flatlanders
sit shoulder to shoulder
and gab over coffee cups that steam
in the humid summer air.
Politics is the topic, but strangers,
wary of strangers, keep their gloves on,
and, although loyalties are revealed,
the sparring is gentle and polite.
There is unity in the freshness of the muffins;
there is division in the headlines.

Few people are out on Main Street at dawn.
Fishermen take shortcuts to the harbor
through neighbors' gardens or friends' boat yards.
All the more opportunity to say good morning.

The cupola on the Monhegan Inn is bathed in
red morning sun,
noticed by the fishermen
on the way to their boats and mentally recorded
as reason to check the barometer
when they get on board.
Everything below the cupola is in the shade
of the far eastern ocean horizon,
just now releasing the sun
for its trip across the sky.

Unlike dawn over a metropolitan city
that tremors with the potential energy
of industry
and commerce
and merchandising
and sin
about to be unleashed with the sun,
dawn on Monhegan's Main Street
moves with the speed of evolution,
the number of people in transit
slowly increasing until by mid-day,
after the ferries have unloaded,
there are as many as six or seven people
with cameras around their necks.
Commerce consists of candy bars
purchased as snacks for the hike
to the headlands.

Main Street on Monhegan,
where intersections are identified
by the tree on the corner,
the garden gate on the north side of the road,
the community bulletin board
"just before the Trailing Yew."

As the sun rises over Monhegan Island,
time settles in like a tired tourist,
and the past, the island matriarch,
sitting on a ledge overlooking the harbor,
nods her welcome
to another day on Main Street.

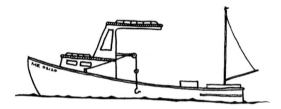

From the Heart

EINSTEIN ON TIME

Someone told me once that
Einstein thought
time is a variable.
That is to say that time is not a constant.
Are you following this?
I think Einstein was right.

When I was a child, a year was a YEAR!
Now a year is a week.
When I was a child, a week was a whole bunch of days
of limitless possibilities,
so numerous that I planned ahead
only as far as the afternoon.
Now a week is a few meetings
interspersed with frenetic activity
that I have apparently convinced myself is important.
Never mind enjoying the moment.
Never mind stopping to smell the roses.

Yesterday, a lifetime was forever,
immeasurable,
like a light year.
But today, swirling in a mix of tomorrows and yesterdays,
a light year is comprehendible,
measurable
and finite.

But let's not talk cosmic stuff.
Let's not throw in big words to impress.

If Einstein was right,
and I think he was,
where is the throttle?
How do I slow this thing down?

THE TREASURE OF THE PRESENT

I had Black Angus cattle once.
That was long ago.
I raised honey bees then.
(They all died.)

I woke to a rooster's reveille,
fed the cows in the dark before dawn,
carried newborn calves
from mid-pasture,
where they were dropped,
to the barn and the warmth of a heater lamp.
That was years ago.

I cut ten cords of pulpwood
into furnace size lengths,
split it,
hauled it to the basement,
stacked it,
nursed the furnace all winter,
heating the house and the hot water.
That was years ago.

I drove cedar fence posts every ten feet,
strung barbed wire around the five acre pasture,
rigged electric fencing when the barbs were ignored,
rounded up my cattle from my neighbor's corn field
in September when the pasture was thin.
That was long ago.

I walked behind Mr. Patrick's farm truck,
heaving hay bales up in the heat of July,
threw them from truck to elevator,
stacked them in hay dust that clung to my sweat,
jumped in the Ellis fully clothed to cool off
and celebrate another field in the barn.
That was years ago.

I coached Little League baseball,
was father to a den of Cub Scouts,
traveled with my love to England,
weekended in New York to see some shows,
drove to Toronto for Shakespeare,
worked full time,
raised two wonderful kids.
That was a long time ago.

I don't .....
I can't do those things now.
But I know that,
in time,
even now
will be long ago.

A KNOCK AT THE DOOR

A knock at the door, late morning.
The dog makes a racket, but the two stand their ground.
They are on God's business.

I know before I open the door what
they have to say — that God is the answer.
I pull the door open, try to be pleasant,
(but, please, don't talk too long).
Two women, earnest, polite, sincere.
(There is a message simply in their manner.)

They ask if I am worried about where
the world is headed.
I answer, yes, I am.
They ask if I read the Bible.
I answer, no, I don't.
They ask if I believe in God.
I answer, yes, I do.

And then I become infused with
the same spirit that brought them to my door.
I say that I believe there is only one God,
worshipped in many ways,
called by many names.
I say that the God they worship
and the god I worship
are the same God.
They doubt that might be true.

They say if I am worried about
the future of the world,
there are answers in the Bible.
I say there are answers in the Koran,
the Bagadva Gita, the poems of Whitman.
God, I say, is the god of all
and the word of God, therefore,
is found in many places.

There is no language
that God does not speak.

They say people should turn to God
to solve the problems of the world
instead of turning to "man."
I say that God works through man,
that the problems of the world
can be solved only by "man," BUT
only if God wants them solved.
They read me something from the Bible.

Then it dawns on me: I am doing
what they came to do;
we are saying different things
but the same things;
God called them to my door,
just as God called me to speak
instead of ushering them
on their way.

After the door is closed, I reflect:
There are people in the world
who bring their beliefs to other people's doors
with guns and machetes in their hands.
These two gentle souls shared their hearts
and listened to me.

Wouldn't the world be Eden itself
if we,
Christians and Muslims,
Jews and Penacostals,
Catholics and Orthodox,
all went door to door from time to time
and had conversations like this?

"Blessed are the peace makers,
for they shall inherit the Kingdom of God."

Oh, that we realize the door
to God's kingdom is the one upon which
visitors knock.

THE ROPED BED

Way down at the end of the roof gable
in the attic space above the upstairs bedrooms
we found the parts of an old roped bed
lying across the ceiling joists.
It must have been in that dark chamber
for a century, maybe more.
Crudely shaped, painted with the red paint
from the paint mine that used to sit
on the sharp bend of the Old County Road,
it is amazingly sturdy if we get the rope
tight enough.

What event in the history of the family that built this farm
led to the bed's emtombment?
Was the bed put away in grief?
Upon news that their son had fallen at Gettysburg?
That their daughter
had died in childbirth
in a sod house in Nebraska?
The disappearance of a son
in the gold fields of Alaska?
Was it in 1917,
a letter from the
commanding officer of their son's unit in France?
There is an aura of mystery about this bed.

But there is more —
Having emerged out of the time capsule
that the inaccessible attic space above the ceiling rafters
in an old farm house becomes,
the bed is an inanimate version of Rip Van Winkle
who woke from a quarter century-long nap
to discover a world he did not recognize.
How the world has changed since this bed
last saw daylight:
Electricity, telephone, television,
automobiles, airplanes, rockets, the great civil war in America,

Wilson's dream of a league of nations,
the rise and destruction of Nazism,
and communism, and
the ascendance of democracy throughout the world;
cures and vaccines for smallpox, infection,
polio, tuberculosis;
computers and nuclear weapons.
It is a new world.

But is it a better world?
There is something about the age
in which this bed was created
that gives it a patina of treasure,
of inestimable value and worth.
Like a family patriarch who lives
well beyond the usual number of years
granted to most humans,
this bed represents years of personal history
that we will never know, but which
glows from this bed like a halo.

Set up in the guest room with dust ruffle and spread,
it radiates an era now gone,
reminding us that continuity in human lives
is often derived from the material things
passed from generation to generation.
Fresh from the darkened attic rafters,
this bed ties us to the past and to the
unknown events in another family's life
about which we can only dream.

WHAT IS IT ABOUT A DOG?

What is it about a dog,
these almost-half-human animals
who choose us over
their own kind?
Is it the look in the eyes?
The silent pledge of loyalty
and holy commitment?

Is it the shy but determined approach toward
the hand of a stranger, held out for inspection and approval,
the obvious desire to please?
Is it the joyful ecstacy that pours from
the face,
the happy canine grin,
the wild exuberance of a tail out of control
when the master returns or
the leash is pulled from the closet?

Was there ever a creature more forgiving,
willing to accept responsibility
for whatever is wrong in your life
that prompted that unfair
reproof and harsh word of rejection?

Does anyone else read your body language
as accurately?
Are the heavy thoughts in your head
as apparent to anyone else
as they are to your dog,
who always knows what you are feeling
and who always offers support
with a nudge of the arm
or a wet love swipe with the tongue?

What do you suppose happened in God's world
that gave him the idea to create a dog?

Loyal friend, loving companion,
ever present attendant who offers
love without boundaries,
devotion without reason.

A dog is a gift.

ONE MOMENT, ONE LIFETIME

A poem for Ann

There is a girl I love who sits for a portrait
with her sister and mother,
whose head of dark curls and gray eyes
and serious gaze would have entrapped me even then,
though a boy of only seven.

There is a girl I love who stands with the cheerleaders,
whose slender waist
and vibrant aura and
occasional glances my way
act as propane lighters
of my seventeen year-old's fire.

There is a girl I love who stops in the morning
at the pool where I work to return my watch
I left on the counter.
(Any excuse will do.)
Brief words.
As I kiss her goodbye (until tonight)
I touch her side
and feel the summer warmth of her skin
through the paisley cotton dress.
The memory of that touch lasts through the day —
through the years.

There is a girl I love who comes down the aisle on the arm of her father,
who smiles at me
and looks in my eyes
as she vows to be mine,
and who dances with me
on that night of wonder
for the very first time.

There is a girl I love who makes me her life,
who nurtures my joys at her breast.
She does the mundane things that make a home,
revels in the laughter of children,
consoles me when my dog is put down,
needles me about my tractors.

There is a girl I love who loves me back,
who remembers with me falling off the bed making love
and laughs with me years later.
There is a bond between us that the years have cemented,
a grafting of souls and minds into one
that began before we knew each other
and that will live forever.

There is a girl I love (who claims to be in her 60's)
who is all of these things to me
in one glance,
one moment,
one lifetime.

There is a girl I love who loves me back.
"Joy" doesn't do this feeling justice.
Words don't work.
One look reveals all that words might say.

There is a girl I love who is life to me,
my treasure,
mirror of my being.

OCTOBER IS MY LATE MIDDLE AGE

October is my late middle age.
In my mid 60's,
the end of the trip somewhere around the corner,
one final burst of living before dormancy sets in.
(Is that what happens? Dormancy?)
November is usually stark, and wet and cold.
I'll probably start having dark thoughts
once I get to November.
I'll have to think my way out of them.
But November is also prelude to celebration.
The darkness seems to lift when I begin December,
even though outside it's darker still.
I've always looked forward
to the end of December,
the celebration of leaving the old
and moving on to new.
But since it's October already,
December is looking different.
Not sure now what the new will be,
I'm staying open minded…..
and hopeful.

October certainly is lovely.

MEN TALKING TO MEN

Take twenty-five men of various shapes
and degrees of hair on their heads,
tell them they can't wear their heavy L.L. Bean hiking boots
or their black-soled work boots
so they have to
slide around in stocking feet or slippers,
put them someplace where their children and wives are not,
and some of the "man" stuff starts to slough off.

Ask each one to "tell us a little about who you are,"
place in his hand a magical stick that requires
he tell the truth.
Each one begins to ask himself as he ponders what to say,
"Well, who am I, really?"
Each one begins to see in his heart things
long ago buried,
feelings long denied,
resolutions long ignored.
And as the circle turns and the talking stick is passed
from man to man, one man's revelation of who he is sparks
another man's realization that he is too,
and the brotherhood of men begins to grow.

Place drums of myriad sizes and shapes and colors
in an open space
and make them available to any man
who feels likes beating out a feeling in rhythm,
and they congregate and watch at first,
and then, when others are
finishing their meals or doing the dishes,
they wander back
and sit down
and give it a tentative slap.

And someone joins them, all new at this,
but all getting the hang of it.
And as the numbers grow, the rhythm picks up,
the sweat starts to flow, the floor starts to bounce,
and they aren't new at this any more.
This is a hell of a lot of fun!

Tell them that the evening program is going to
consist of any talent they would like to share,
any story they would like to tell,
any poem they would like to recite,
any song they would like to sing.
Ask them to sign up on the program sheet.
And immediately some extrovert jumps to list his offering,
and others think of reasons why they won't.
But slowly the list grows,
and someone who thought he'd sit it out
begins to think, like the drumming,
What the hell, I'll give it a try.
And when the program begins, these twenty-five men
sit like kindergartners in a classroom,
mesmerized by the joy and sadness and exuberance and
unleashed and unrefined and unabashed honest confessions
of men sharing who they are and lighting up the room with
their awakened spirit.

Bring them together at the end of the weekend,
and pass the stick that requires the truth.
The stick is now superfluous.
Inhibitions have fled; truth is all there is to say.

"Tell us about who you are."
No need. You have seen who I am.
You have freed who I am.

MY MOTHER'S VOICE

I don't ever remember wondering if a voice
I faintly heard was my mother's voice or not.
I always knew.
Just as the fledgling albatross can pick out its
mother from the thousands of look-alikes
that cling to the same rock,
I could pick out my mother's voice
in a crowd of hundreds.

Before I could talk or walk,
long before I was consciously piecing the world together,
my mother's voice was as integral to my world
as the thunder of the surf is to the sea.
The sound of comfort, security and unconditional acceptance,
my mother's voice was the serenade of my childhood,
the song that began and ended each day.

Mom is now in her twilight years,
and the sun in my heaven
is slipping toward the horizon.
But I suspect that when Mom is gone, I will still hear that sound.
And when I too return to the eternal soul of the universe
I will be enveloped by my mother's voice
which was,
and is,
and always will be
the sound of love.

DON'T GO

A father's lament

Don't go, little one.
Continue to believe that every smile you see
is from a heart that loves you.
Hold your little doll
as if your love gives it life.
Believe that it thrives on your devotion,
and that it dreams like you.

Don't go.
Talk to the dog as to a brother.
Ponder a snowflake as proof of miracles.
Look upon summer as an endless season of adventure.
Trust that your mother and I will love
each other as much as we love you.
Don't go.

Listen to stories with a belief that they are true.
Share in the joy of your friends;
hurt when they hurt.
Find goodness where I no longer can.
Don't go.

The sparkle in your eyes reflects my heaven.
The love in your laughter is my god's whisper.
You are all the proof I need.

Don't go.

FATHER AND SON

Next year my son will be forty.
I try to envision those years moving backwards in time,
squeezing my memory, like a ketchup bottle.
But all I get is a table spoon or so of soundless pictures.

I long for movies of our hikes together,
even just short "specials" of our manly excursions
in boat and canoe,
"hunting" partridge,
never expecting to see one,
let alone shoot one,
just relishing being together.

I try to shake out onto the table
all the soccer games and canoe races
when I was a spectator,
not of the event,
but of my son rising to the challenge of competition,
and basking with pride simply because
of the way he carried himself.
I didn't care if they won, really.
Just his being in the game was as good as a win.

I try to list the things we did as companions,
and all I get out of the bottle are freeze frames
of images devoid of the emotion of the moment,
still life paintings of just seconds in time
that were stamped into my memory
without the emotional sound track.

Forty years is a hodge podge of pictures,
like the pile of photographs in the corner
of the desk,
waiting for one of us to sort into piles
by year or subject in an effort to put our history
into some kind of order.

But neither of us tackles the task,
and pictures of the past slip
from the bottom to the middle,
dislodging others.
And over the years, the history of our lives
as a family
becomes a jumble of unconnected images
that will eventually be stuffed into a big manila folder,
to be discovered by someone cleaning out
the desk drawer after we've gone.

So, to heck with it.
I live in the present, knowing that
the love between father and son
has been carved in our hearts
by now forgotten things we did together
and aware that,
even without the picture history,
we still have excursions to take,
politics to debate,
lives to live, and
love to share.

THE LITTLE GIRL IN THE CANOPY BED
On my daughter's 37th birthday

"I have a daughter!" I said to myself.
"She's tiny. My god! She's tiny!"
But already she has a special look on her face
that says,
"We're going to do this my way."

I have a three-year-old daughter
who delights in feminine things.
Her room should reflect her gender (I think):
a canopy bed, pink dust ruffle and spread,
miniature kitchen in the corner
where her dolls can be fed.

I have a territorial eight-year-old daughter
whose room is off limits to her brother.
(At this age, doorways delineate domains.)
But there are times when
strictures are loosened and
boundaries ignored
and the two of them become friends.

I have a beautiful daughter who can sing and compute
and write and compete with the best,
but, with confidence lacking
and unsure of herself,
she's reluctant to take the world by the tail.
But she knows who she is and refuses to hide.
In time, the right person
will see the diamond
beneath the thin layer of doubt.

I now have a daughter who is second to none
as a mother and woman of values,
who handles her daughters with love and compassion,
is advisor at times to her dad
and her mother's best friend.

I have a daughter who's grown
from a child into a woman.
I've watched this transformation with
wonder,
pride,
love
and admiration
for the courage of
the little girl
in the canopy bed.

I WILL WIN

It begins as nothing more than
a feeling that something is wrong.
(Wonderful, how the body talks to you.)
At first, there are things I can't identify.
Then, reaching for a napkin, I see it —
a hitch,
a ratcheting of my unfolding arm
as I extend it across the table.

Sitting on his examination stool,
the doctor wheels over to
look me in the eye.
"Mr. Nye, you have Parkinson's disease."

It doesn't register.
"Parkinson's is a chronic, progressive disease...."
Is he talking about me?
A chronic disease.
It has no cure?
A progressive disease.
It will get worse?
It doesn't register . . . at first.

When it does, there is no future.
Nothing is fun.
What's the point?

But in time I learn that
feeling sorry for myself
doesn't make me feel any better;
that there is
absolutely
nothing
I can do
to make it go away.

So I learn to live with it,
live around it,
ignore it,
occasionally tell it to go do something
obscene,
show it off and then put it to shame.
It's like living with a roommate
I can't stand.

And I learn that the only way
to win
is to treat it as if I couldn't care less,
to concede lost ground but to shrug it off,
to use it as a lesson in biology and anatomy,
and as evidence of the miracle
of the human body.

And I also learn that my world,
even with Parkinson's,
is gloriously full
of family and friends,
love and devotion,
beauty wherever I look,
joy,
and, always and everywhere,
nature's wonders.

This is not a battle of the flesh.
This is a battle of the spirit.

So, as the years move along
and my chronic, progressive companion
continues to wheedle his way into my life,
I will adjust
with a shrug.

And I will win.

I'LL NEVER GROW OLDER THAN MY DAD

As the years go by and I get older,
I am beginning to realize that
I'll never grow older than my dad.
He died when he was fifty-seven.
I am now sixty-two.
Before he died, he seemed to me to be old.
I am five years older.
But I don't think I will ever be older than my dad.

I still occasionally dream about him.
In those dreams he's always older than I.
(I can't even dream a different relationship.
My heart will not allow it.)

When I look at pictures of him,
I unconsciously place myself below his head,
even though I am now the same height as he.
I could live to be ninety-six, but when I die and
return to the source of all things of the heart,
he will greet me as the father,
I will be the son, and the relationship will resume
and the roles will stay the same.
I won't be ninety-six then.
He won't be fifty-seven.
We will be what we have always been —
father and son.

So, as the years go by and I grow older,
I ponder this transcendence of spirit over time,
and I am
comforted.

MY FATHER'S THINGS

My dad died 28 years ago.
I still have some of his things:

A red plaid Pendleton bath robe.
(I look like Dad in that thing now.)

An old Sears table saw bought used in 1950.
I still use it, (but for rough cuts only).

An old grinding wheel, noisy as sin,
but sharpens mower blades in no time.

Trays and trays of screws and nuts,
sorted in biscuit pans by size.
(Just stir and search.)

His gold watch given to him in '57.
It hasn't worked for years.
It's going to cost too much to fix it,
so I keep it in my drawer.

I had his pocket knife but lost it.
(I always lose my pocket knife.)

There are other things of his I have as well:

I have his feet. I swear, my feet look just like his.

I have his eyes. (They're big and brown.)

I have his gait (knees kicking out like bow-legged cowboys).
When I walk in front of storefront windows, it's my dad.

I have some other things of his too:

A love of animals,
especially dogs,
one of God's greatest inventions.

His value system and code of conduct,
the do's and don'ts of being a man.

Some might say, "Bathrobes and saws and codes of conduct
are not exactly jewels to take to the bank."

I answer, "Jewels don't shine as brightly as my father's things."

"LET'S GO FOR A RIDE"

I get the same response that I've always gotten:
a look of excitement and joy,
immediate effort to rise and head for the car.
But rising is now a major project,
and jumping up into the
back seat is not possible.
So I lift him up, moving mechanically,
trying to drive my grief and dread down into my gut.

How many times have I said, "Let's go for a ride"?
The sunroof was for him so he could stand
on the center console and poke his huge head up   .
through the roof and survey the passing world
like a tank commander.
I got a kick out of people smiling and pointing
when they saw him.
No smile for him, though.
Piloting this tank is serious business.

But no more tank commander trips, now.
Legs are too wobbly.

He just lazes on the back seat,
enjoying being with me.
I talk to him and get the usual unspoken
"I don't have any idea what you are talking about,
but I love you anyway" look.

White hair around the face now,
eyes glazed with age.
Even though he can barely see,
he'll go wherever I go.
That's been his life purpose.

My hands shake on the wheel
as I contemplate our farewell.

Only a little while back he was an armful of puppyness,
for years a constant companion and playmate,
always striving to do what I wanted him to do.
Snuggling down on my feet under the desk,
he wanted to be close.

So I owe him this last trip,
when he is still a dignified presence
in the backseat.
We'll park the car, I'll put the leash on him
and help him down.
And, when he recognizes where we are,
he'll begin to shake like he always does.
But, like a trooper, he'll go wherever I go.

I will miss him so.

BIRTHDAY

Today is the day.
I'm eleven today.
I think I'm getting a brand new bike.
I've been checking the closets and the attic
and on top of the secretary in the dining room
and I haven't seen anything that looks like a birthday present.
I think it's going to be a bike.
Gee, I hope it's a bike.

At breakfast this morning,
Mom gave me a kiss and wished me a happy birthday.
Then she said something very important.
I think this is very significant.
She said, "We'll have a surprise for you when you get home."

Now she wouldn't have said that if I was getting
new pajamas or something like that.
There is something big in this.
I think it's a bike.
Gee, I hope it's a bike.

Lunch in the cafeteria on your birthday.
Nobody knows it's my birthday.
I don't want them to know.
I wish the day would move along faster.
Have you noticed how time seems to move slower
when you want it to move faster?

I'm getting worried.
The last time Mom said they'd have a surprise for me
when I got home,
I got a baby sister.

This bus ride is taking forever.
Why does the bus driver have to wait until
every kid walks into the house and the door is shut?
You'd think people didn't have anything else to do

than to watch kids amble home.
Gee, I hope it's a bike.

Wait a minute.
There's something leaning against the front steps.

Yes!

MAKING LOVE

As years go by and passions cool,
we make love in places that
young lovers only dream about.

We make love at the kitchen table,
a Scrabble board the mattress
and hints to help the other
our passionate kisses.

We make love in the car,
thrilling to beautiful scenery
or a rarely seen wild animal.

We make love in front of the fireplace,
watching a game show,
sharing our latest craft creations.

We make love on the middle school hockey field,
proudly watching our granddaughter
dribble the ball down the field
with half the opposing team
in hot pursuit.

We make love in the bathroom,
where I marvel at the beauty of my
companion and friend of so many years
and tell her as she lathers all over
that she is the prettiest girl I know.

We make love in bed with our pajamas on,
she curled up against me, spoon on spoon,
feeling each other's warmth and whispering before falling into
sleep,
"I love you."

We are so shamelessly promiscuous,
we make love in church, for god's sake,
sharing the hymnal hand on hand,
touching during prayers to say to the other
without words or looks,
"You are the rock of my happiness."

Wonderfully, heavy breathing is still
in our repertoire.

But the bond between us that challenges even death
is the love made here and there,
time and time again,
side by side.

THE CONNECTION

A poem for my granddaughter Kate's 12th birthday

An infant,
cooing at whatever face smiles down on you,
you don't really know me.
I could be a mobile
hanging over your crib.

In time, you know you've
seen me before,
but there is no real connection.
I'm a nice old person who seems to like you a lot,
but when I leave,
there is no sadness.

And then one day,
soon after you are walking,
I'm on the living room floor,
painting the baseboard heat trim.
You come strolling in from the kitchen,
Baby Santa Clause in your arms,
stop when you see me on the floor,
smile shyly and say,
"Hi, Granddad."
I say, "Hi, Katie."

Our first conversation,
one of the most memorable of any in my life.

I will never forget it.

JENNY ROBIN

A poem for my granddaughter Jennifer on her 11th birthday

People might think the birth
of a second granddaughter
is not as exciting as the first.
They would be wrong.
Another new life to become a part of ours,
another little one to watch absorb the world,
see the wheels turning in her head
as she encounters, catalogs and computes
objects she has never seen before.

A chance to watch her timidly test the feel
of a puddle of dry leaves in which her
older sister is swimming.

The thrill of watching this three year old respond
to the question, "How much is 9 plus 9?"
with three minutes of intensely thoughtful silence
in the back seat of the car
followed by
"eighteen."

The thrill of reading her poems,
composed as easily as writing her name,
when she's only seven.

The joy of seeing her, already a teacher,
conduct class with her dolls,
all of whom pay rapt attention,
secure in their belief that the teacher
loves them.

Who says number two isn't as much fun?
Who else is going to canoe with me?
Ride bikes with me?
Play cards with me?

Two granddaughters is exactly twice as much fun,
and twice as much love,
as one.

IF I SHOULD DIE (and I will someday)

If I should die,
(and I will some day),
I won't be far away.
You will see me.

When the big golden retriever ambles in
and lies down under the kitchen table,
he's lying at my feet.
I'm in the chair.
When Ann throws the covers off
and heads for the warm bathroom,
I'm in the dressing room, up and ready to go.
I'm watching the birds at the feeder.
I'm waiting for the tulips to bloom
and the flowering shrubs to burst in color.
I'm down in the barn, fiddling with the old tractor.
Where ever I used to be, I am still there.
What ever I used to do, I still do it.
You will see me.

If I should die,
(and I will some day),
I hope, when it happens,
that I'm still in the game.
When I was a boy I would day dream of being
carried out on a stretcher while the cheerleaders wept.
And, of course,
I would return to the conflict
to even greater glory.
I can't expect to return to play,
but the game has been such fun,
I won't leave right away.
I'm still here.
You will see me.

My life has been a joyful banquet;
plenty of frosting and cake,
delectable appetizers and
nourishing and filling main courses.
(Note the order of the servings.)
Many friends at our table to share the feast,
some still on the guest list,
some having moved on.

Where I sat, I am still sitting.
Where I worked, I am still there.
I am with those I love,
I am with my family.
I am with my dog.
I am with my friends.

No, I am too much a part of all of these things.
If I should die,
(and I will some day)
I won't be far away.
You will see me.

RELIGION IN THE RIBBONS

"Christ is born! Alleluia!"
"Only ten shopping days until Christmas!"
We lament tying one to the other,
but this is not naked materialism.
There is religion in the ribbons.

A wintry night.
A tiny baby,
a cattle stall,
a bed in the hay,
two thousand years ago.
From hundreds of miles Kings come to present gifts
to the child of a pauper.
Shepherds, for whom birthing is part of the job,
stand in awe of the miracle of creation.
Something special here.

There is love in the mother's eyes,
wonder in the faces of the magi,
celebration in the star-studded sky,
hope in the hearts of the shepherds.

The shopping frenzy is not without heart.
Toys celebrate children.
People don't load up with gifts for others
because they have to.
Presents hidden by lovely wrappings
are mysteries that
speak of love,
engender joy,
reaffirm family,
encourage giving.

Christmas decorations and holiday foods,
annual trips to the homestead,
memories of lifetimes together,
reflections of lives lived fully,
love for those present
and aching longing for those gone.

Time to pause and reflect.
There is sadness mixed with wonder and joy,
awareness of the passing years
when we marvel at how the kids have grown
and then realize that
time didn't stop for us either.

Christmas —-
family,
children,
infants,
birth,
innocence,
redemption,
rebirth.
The infusion of divine soul in human flesh,
presented to us as a baby—
as every baby, everywhere, as long as babies will be born.

Why not celebrate with gifts and food and family?
Let the cash registers ring —
the sound of people in celebration
thinking of others.

"A baby is born. Alleluia!
Let the heavens sing, Alleluia!"
Let us celebrate!

CHRISTMAS EVE

The tree is all set.
Packages piled at its base.
Telephone calls from the kids confirming
the times of dinner and church.
Nothing much left to do.
The Fed Ex guy just delivered the last late order.
I'll wrap it,
and then what?

Time on my hands.
Time to think.

What is this all about?

Christmas is about family,
gathering together to celebrate.
We do this in-gathering every year of our lives,
and come to associate this night
and the days around it
with the people closest to our hearts.
But always there is someone
who is no longer here,
who is still in our hearts but forever gone
from our embraces.

"Through the years,
we all will be together,
if the Fates allow."

What the songwriter doesn't say is
"the Fates will not allow it,"
because we are mortal beings,
and just as we all begin our journeys
as babies adored by mother and admirers,
we all will eventually be aches in the hearts
of those who miss us.
It is Christmas eve when the ache is the worst.

And that is why we turn again to the baby,
to celebrate birth that soothes the aching heart,
that gives us reason to hope and dream,
that reminds us of the miracle of life,
and tells us by this annual gathering of family
that it is our very mortality that makes
life that begins as
a baby
so precious.

Not in spite of, but because of our heartache,
this is a silent and holy night
in which, through adoration of a baby,
we celebrate life.

Acknowledgments

THIS BOOK of poetry would never have seen the light of day in a bookstore or anywhere else if it hadn't been for a number of people.

First and foremost is Jim Furber, the creator of the Emerging Poets web site and the executive director of TJMF Publishing Company. Without his visionary work in bringing aspiring artists together on one internet site to share and critique each other's work, I and many others would still be struggling on our own, looking for support and encouragement. Jim not only created a way for aspiring poets to work together, he courageously embarked on the creation of a publishing arm to get the work of many of those aspiring artists into the public arena. For his dedication, vision and encouragement, I will forever be indebted.

Lorraine Sautner, a colleague on Emerging Poets, has been my mentor ever since I posted my first poem. She sensed there was potential in my early poems, lavished praise and at the same time made gentle suggestions to make them better and me a better poet. Her encouragement, especially early on, was integral to my growth as a poet. She was my chief advisor in the compilation of this book of poems and honored me by writing the preface to the collection. That her name is a part of this tome is a thrill for me.

And there is a group of poets on EP, whom I will not name individually, who have tutored me, cajoled me, tolerated my rambling narratives that go on forever, praised me, and celebrated with me and who have been my artistic family and the supportive home base as I have explored the world of poetic expression. This book is in part theirs. My gratitude for their support and encouragement will never cease.

And, of course, Ann's patience, constant love and support are part of the reason why I started writing poetry and have been part of the reason why I continue to do so.

Ken Nye